1001 Bugs to Spot

Emma Helbrough

Illustrated by Teri Gower

Designed by Natacha Goransky

Edited by Anna Milbourne

Natural history consultants:
Dr. Margaret Rostron and Dr. John Rostron

Contents

Bugs to spot

The pictures in this book show all kinds of places where bugs might be lurking. On every page there are lots of bugs for you to find and count. There are 1001 bugs to spot altogether. The example pages below show you what you need to do to find them all.

Each little picture shows you what to look for in the big picture.

The blue number tells you how many of that bug you need to find.

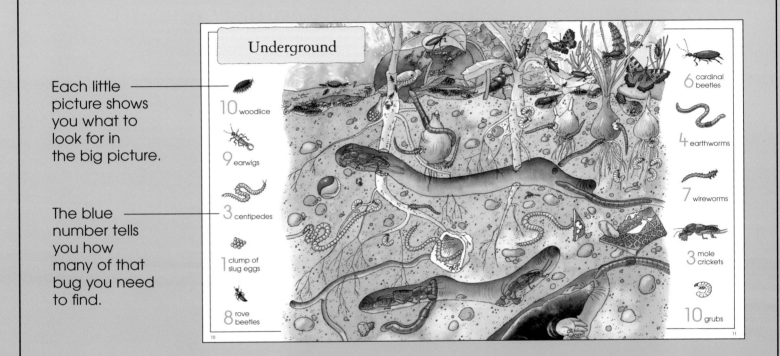

Underground

10 woodlice

9 earwigs

3 centipedes

1 clump of slug eggs

8 rove beetles

6 cardinal beetles

4 earthworms

7 wireworms

3 mole crickets

10 grubs

This is a honeybee.

Honeybees live all over the world. They collect pollen from flowers and use it to make honey. There is a honeybee flying through every big picture in this book. Can you spot them all?

There are lots more things for you to spot on pages 30 to 31.

Flowerbed

9 snails 4 spittlebugs 10 stink bugs 8 pink spiders 6 tiger moths

10 ants
3 hairy caterpillars
9 bumblebees
7 crane flies
5 peacock butterflies

Rocky desert

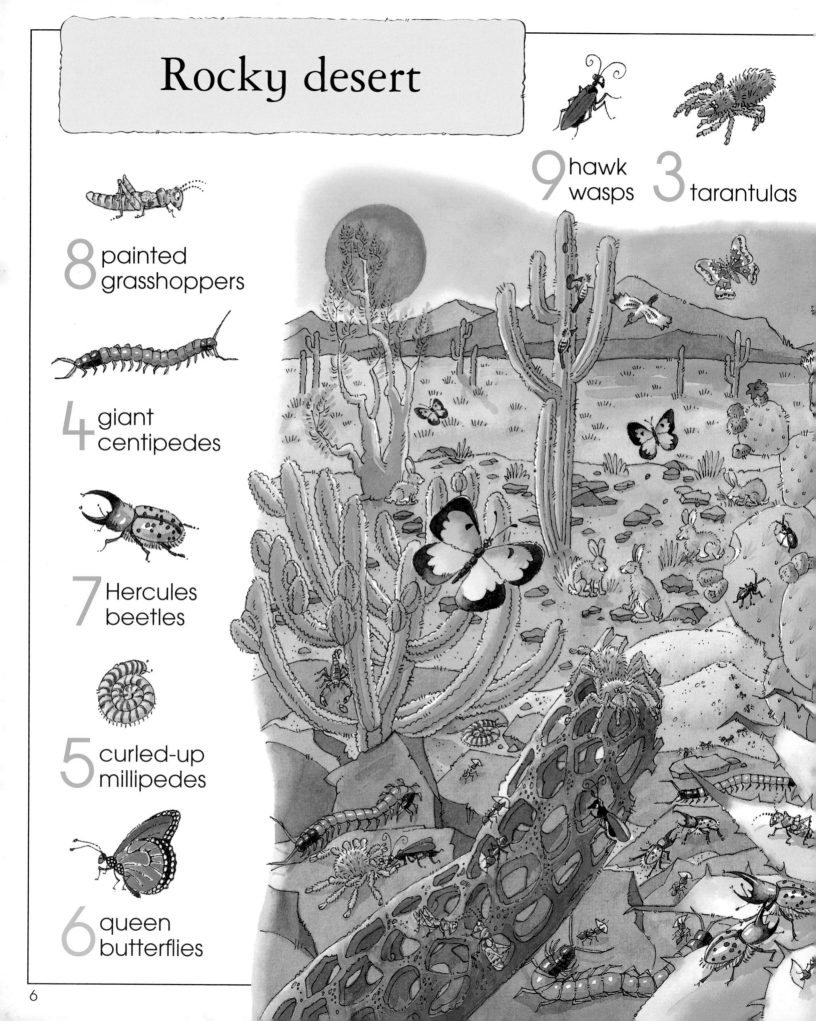

9 hawk wasps

3 tarantulas

8 painted grasshoppers

4 giant centipedes

7 Hercules beetles

5 curled-up millipedes

6 queen butterflies

4 hairy scorpions

10 ants with seeds

9 cactus beetles

Tropical treetops

6 leaf mantises

10 thorn bugs

9 flag-footed bugs

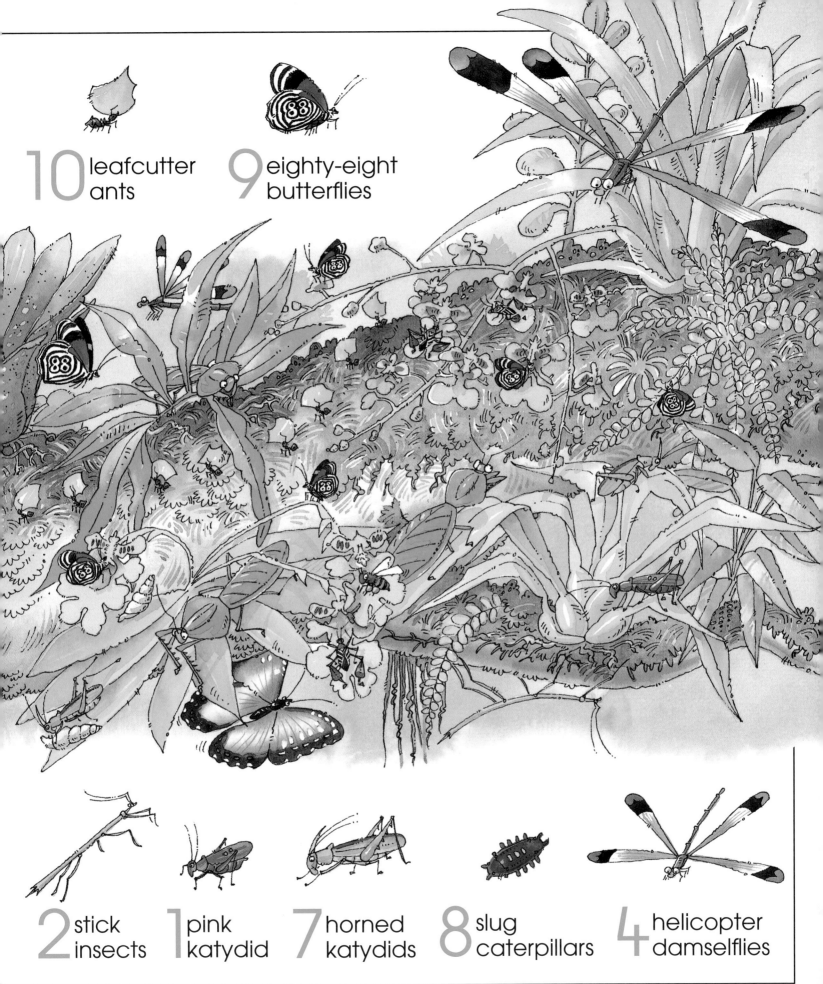

10 leafcutter ants

9 eighty-eight butterflies

2 stick insects

1 pink katydid

7 horned katydids

8 slug caterpillars

4 helicopter damselflies

Underground

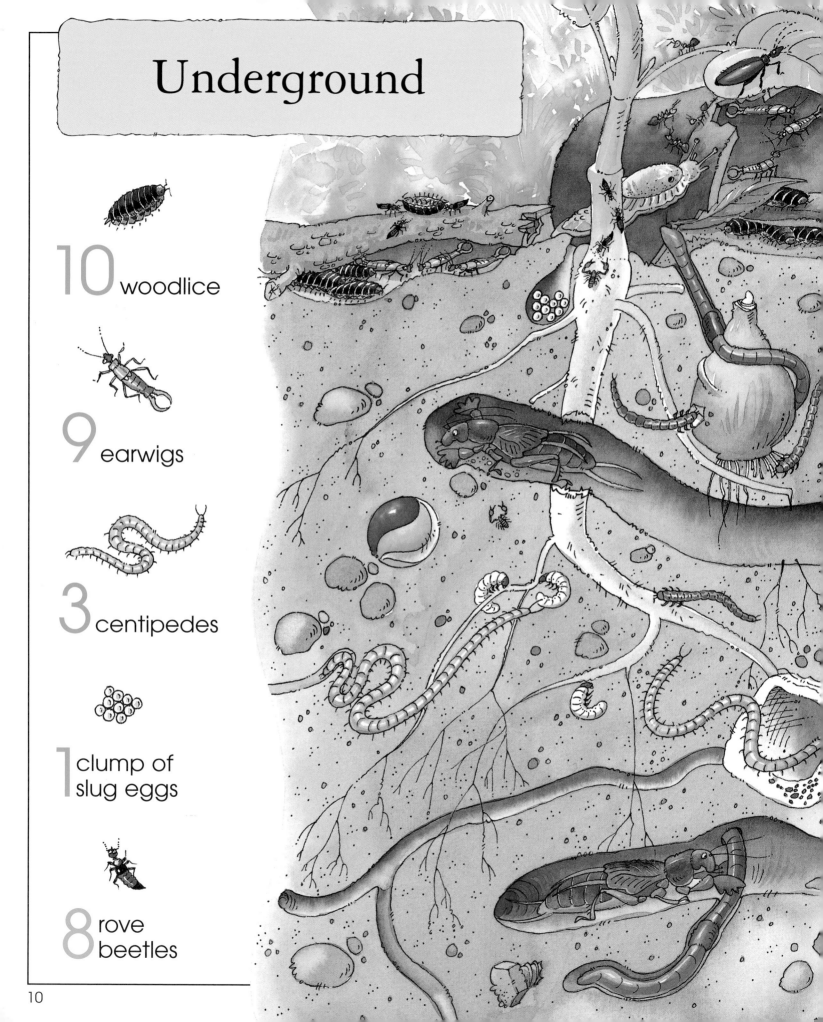

10 woodlice

9 earwigs

3 centipedes

1 clump of slug eggs

8 rove beetles

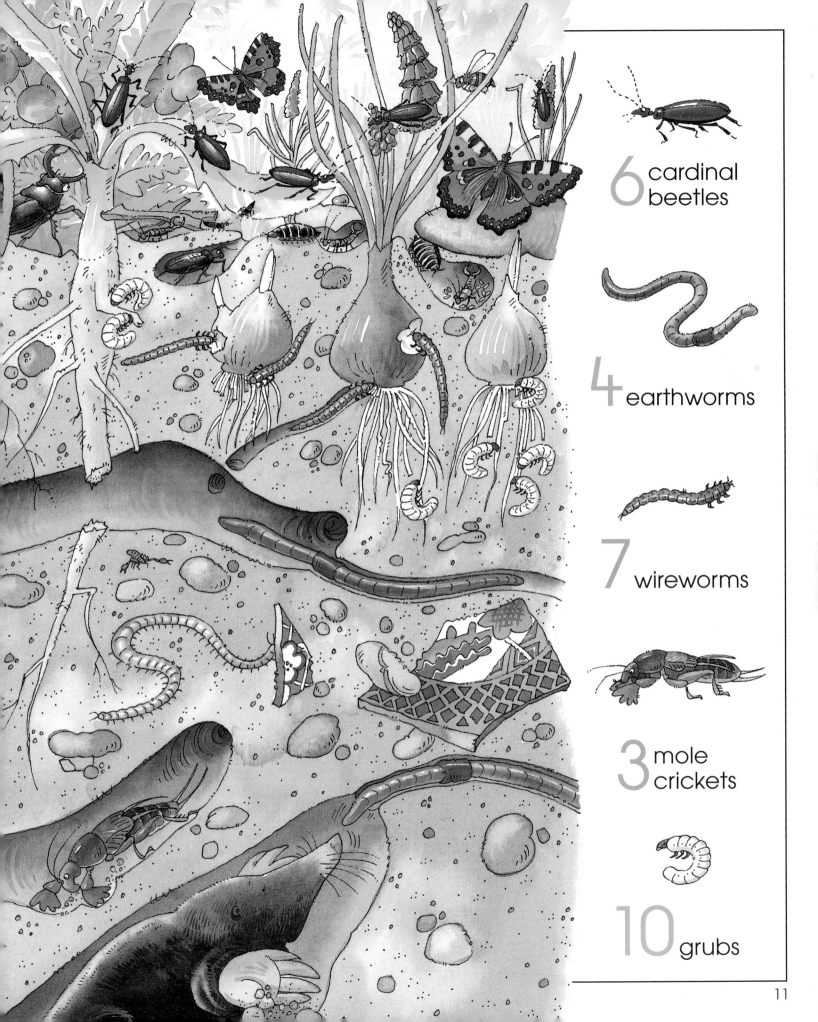

6 cardinal beetles

4 earthworms

7 wireworms

3 mole crickets

10 grubs

Sandy desert

9 desert crickets **10** dune beetles

5 painted lady butterflies

8 long-legged beetles

5 sun spiders

6 dung beetles

9 mosquitoes

10 dune ants

6 thick-tailed scorpions

4 wheel spiders rolling

13

Garden shed

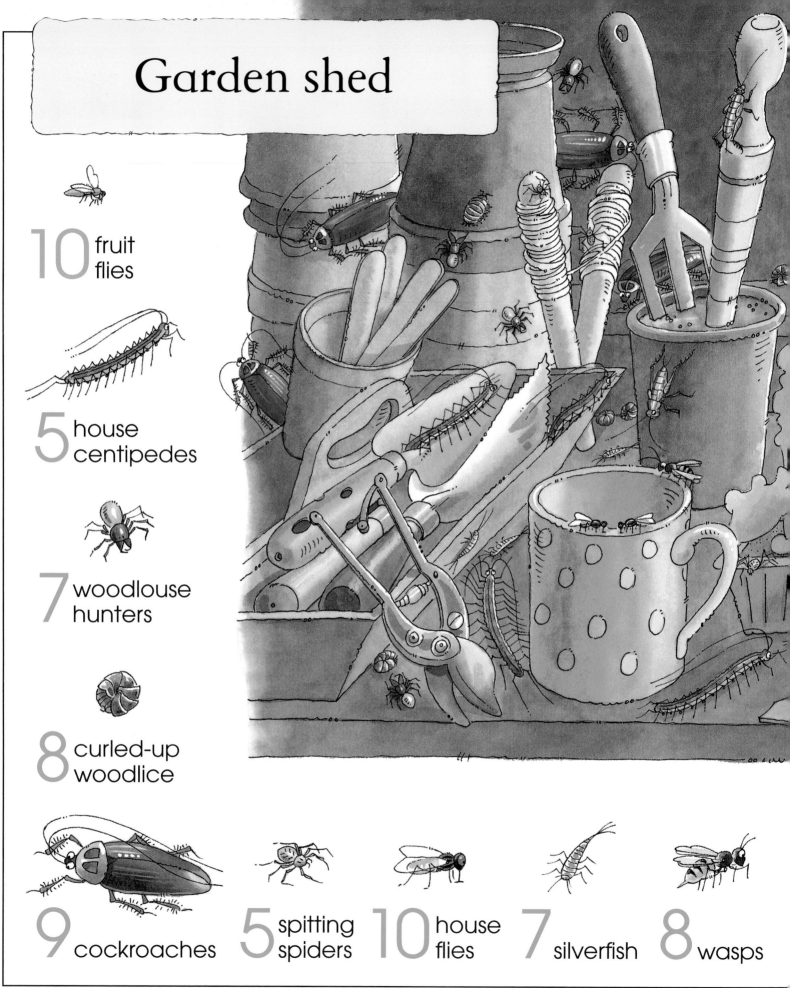

10 fruit flies

5 house centipedes

7 woodlouse hunters

8 curled-up woodlice

9 cockroaches

5 spitting spiders

10 house flies

7 silverfish

8 wasps

6 house
crickets

Jungle floor

7 frog beetles

9 horned spiders

10 pill millipedes

8 longhorn beetles

2 pink dragonflies

9 yellow stink bugs

8 palm weevils

6 lantern bugs

9 stalk-eyed flies

7 harlequin butterflies

Vegetable patch

9 lacewings   3 yellow spiders

7 slugs

10 leaf hoppers

4 striped beetles

10 spotted beetles

5 buckeye butterflies

6 harlequin bugs

8 banded snails

6 looper caterpillars

Leafy woodland

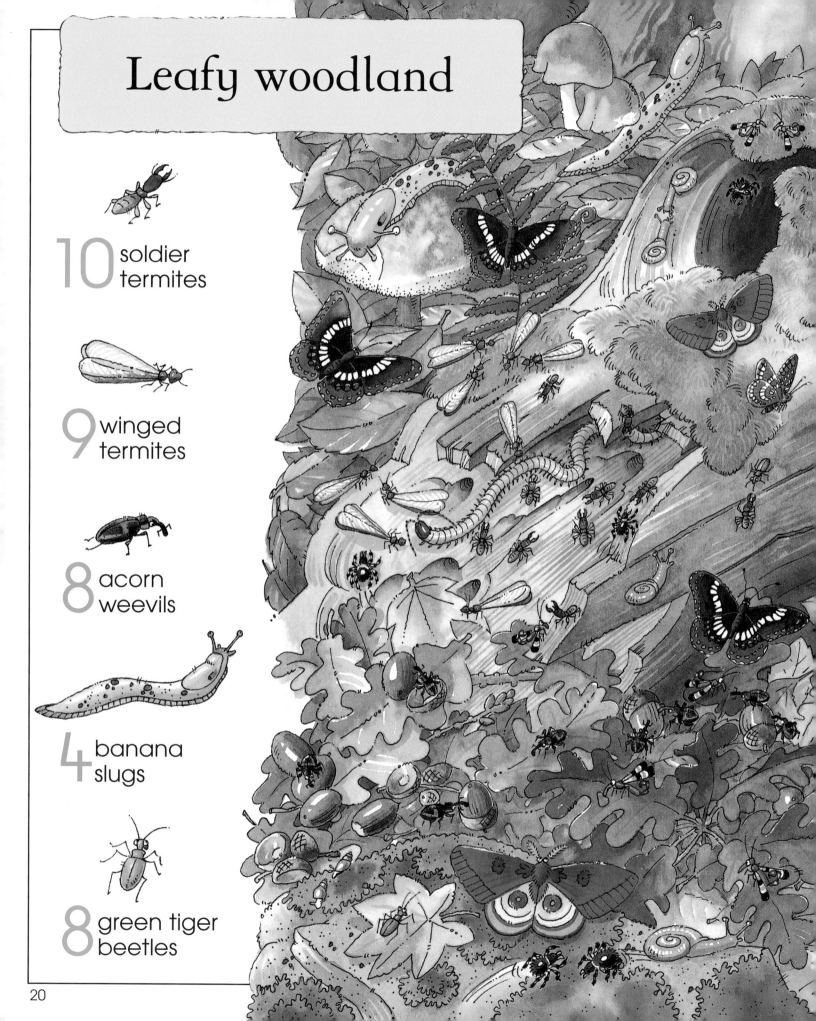

10 soldier termites

9 winged termites

8 acorn weevils

4 banana slugs

8 green tiger beetles

8 flat-disc
snails

6 io
moths

9 fungus
beetles

10 jumping
spiders

7 scorpion
flies

Pond life

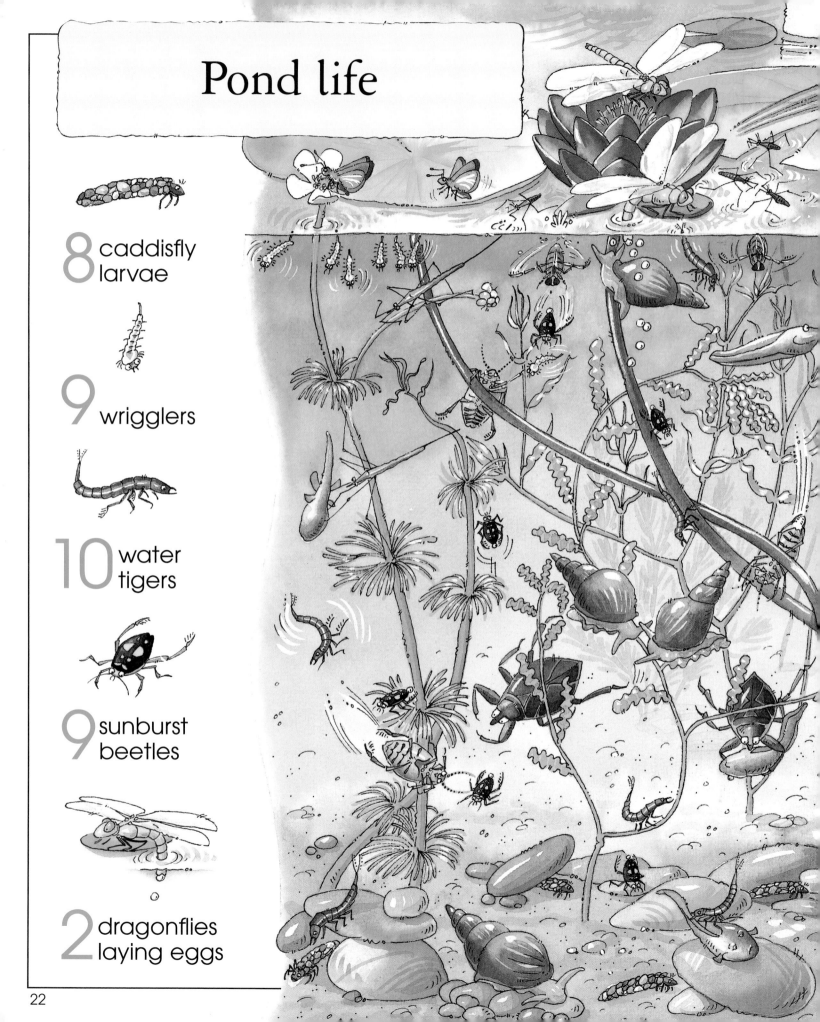

8 caddisfly larvae

9 wrigglers

10 water tigers

9 sunburst beetles

2 dragonflies laying eggs

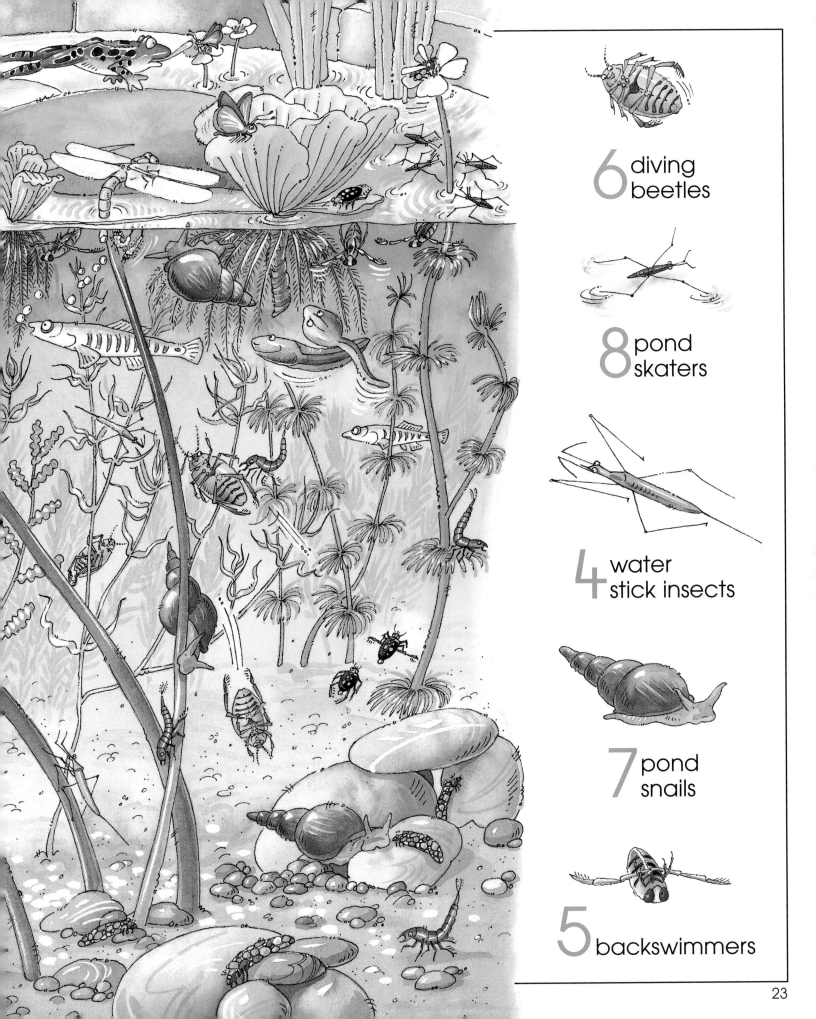

6 diving beetles

8 pond skaters

4 water stick insects

7 pond snails

5 backswimmers

Craggy cave

10 herald moths

10 ground beetles

8 harvestmen

6 cave silverfish

5 giant millipedes

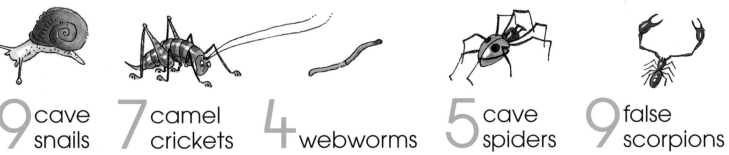
9 cave snails

7 camel crickets

4 webworms

5 cave spiders

9 false scorpions

Grassy meadow

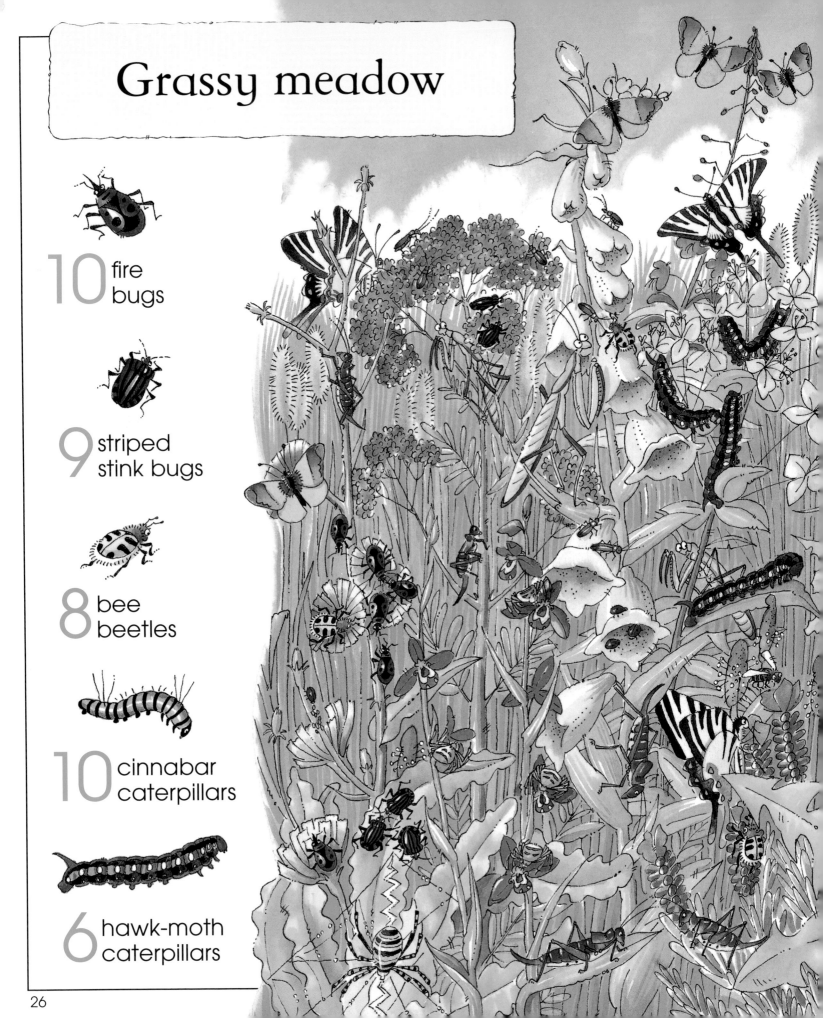

10 fire bugs

9 striped stink bugs

8 bee beetles

10 cinnabar caterpillars

6 hawk-moth caterpillars

5 praying mantises

7 crab spiders

5 wasp spiders

9 bush crickets

7 soldier beetles

27

Nightlife

6 stag beetles   4 cicadas

9 owl moths

10 weaver ants

7 blue beetles

10 fireflies

8 awlking caterpillars

9 snails with yellow shells

3 slant-faced grasshoppers

7 inchworm moths

Butterfly house

At a butterfly house, you can see butterflies from all around the world. Look back through the book and see if you can find and count all of these butterflies.

5 swordtails

4 zebra butterflies

2 blue morpho butterflies

5 sleepy orange butterflies

6 yellow pansy butterflies

8 orange-tips

4 skipper
butterflies

7 swallowtails

2 tortoiseshell
butterflies

5 checkerspots

6 white
admirals

5 comma
butterflies

4 fritillaries

3 brimstones

Answers

Did you find all the butterflies in the book?
Here's where they are.

5 swordtails:
Jungle floor
(pages 16 and 17)

4 zebra butterflies:
Vegetable patch
(pages 18 and 19)

2 blue morpho butterflies:
Tropical treetops
(pages 8 and 9)

5 sleepy orange butterflies:
Rocky desert
(pages 6 and 7)

6 yellow pansy butterflies:
Sandy desert
(pages 12 and 13)

8 orange-tips:
Grassy meadow
(pages 26 and 27)

4 skipper butterflies:
Pond life
(pages 22 and 23)

7 swallowtails:
Grassy meadow
(pages 26 and 27)

2 tortoiseshell butterflies:
Underground
(pages 10 and 11)

6 white admirals:
Leafy woodland
(pages 20 and 21)

5 checkerspots:
Leafy woodland
(pages 20 and 21)

5 comma butterflies:
Flowerbed
(pages 4 and 5)

4 fritillaries:
Garden shed
(pages 14 and 15)

3 brimstones:
Flowerbed
(pages 4 and 5)

Cover design: Josephine Thompson
Managing editor: Gillian Doherty
Managing designers: Laura Fearn
and Mary Cartwright

The publishers would like to thank Carl Cantaluppi,
Horticulture Agent at North Carolina State University
and Dr. Gordon Wardell, President of S.A.F.E. Research
& Development, for their helpful advice.

First published in 2005 by Usborne Publishing Ltd.,
83-85 Saffron Hill, London EC1N 8RT, England.
www.usborne.com